DAD'S
WORDS of
WISDOM

DAVID HORNER

David Horner

June 2006

Dad's Words of Wisdom
© by David Horner 2004

Providence Communications
6339 Glenwood Avenue, Raleigh, NC 27612-2638

All Scripture quotations, unless otherwise indicated, are taken from the
New American Standard Bible © 1960, 1962, 1963, 1968, 1971, 1972,
1973, 1975, 1977 by the Lockman Foundation.

Photo of David Horner, courtesy of
Sam Gray Creative Portrait Design in Raleigh, N.C.

ISBN: 0-9740963-1-8

DEDICATION

To Jeff, Scott and Jon with gratitude that you have all grown up to be men I am proud to call my sons . . .

When the Lord entrusted Cathy and me with three sons, He surely knew what He was doing! These years of growing with each of you have been a delight beyond words. Although we have gone through times of disagreement and expected periods of frustration (you with me and I with you!), I could not have asked for any greater joy than being your dad.

In the following pages, I have attempted to jot down random notes and thoughts on subjects that I thought you needed to know. Most of the ideas are hardly original thinking, nearly none of them pretending to be brilliant insights, but all of them important enough for me to think that it would be helpful if you know them.

In each case, I have tried to reduce the main point to a brief statement as a heading, followed by a note of explanation and a biblical reference point, and then room for you to add your own thoughts as you feel they are appropriate. I pray that this project never ends as I continue to add to these pages as you get married and have children of your own. Growth never ceases, and so I trust that the Lord will always be giving me a chance to watch as you move ahead in your walk with Him. May the Lord Jesus be honored by the way you live, the choices you make and the character you develop for His glory.

I offer you these thoughts with all the love I have and a promise to be there for you all of my life.

PREFACE

Little boys grow up. Dads do their best to prepare them for what they will face as adults, but somehow it never seems to be enough. There is always one more lesson to teach, one more warning to convey, one more value to instill, until eventually our little boys become young men and are on their way.

As the father of three sons, I have my share of regrets about the things I never got around to telling them. With everyone going in different directions once they reached the teen years, sometimes my wife Cathy and I felt we had achieved a major success if everyone was home for a meal together. Sure, we talked about sitting down with each one of our sons and making sure we had adequately prepared them to be responsible, independent young men when it was time for them to leave home. But so many random thoughts never did find their way into words.

If you talked with my sons, I doubt they would tell you they were deprived in any way, but I always had just a couple more things I wanted to say but never seemed to get around to it. They are remarkable young men whose lives tell their own stories of lessons well learned, values embraced, and skills fine-tuned. With good friends, high standards, and solid goals in life, I must say that I am delighted with what they have become and filled with hope for what they still will be.

Yet in order to make sure that I did not let them down, I started several years ago on a project that continues still. I began to write down the things I wanted to be sure they knew from me, things I believe are important for a Christian man to know to be able to make a significant difference for Christ with his life. I have come to refer to these random pieces of advice as "just one more thing" because that tends to be the way we have talked about life during their growing up years. Those last pieces of advice as they were getting ready for a date, those quick words of last-minute counsel as they were heading out the door—"Just one more thing before you go . . ."

Collecting these insights and sayings has probably been more beneficial to me than it has to my boys, but I feel better knowing that they at least have this much in their hands as they go out into the world.

Are you ready for some real honesty? I wish I had gone over these topics individually with each of my sons. Instead of weekly times with me to go over this stuff, they got the book, all compiled and neatly bound together. What I am putting in your hands is a plan with some content I believe in and that is biblically based. What I cannot give you is the determination to do whatever it takes to spend quality time with a young man God has entrusted to your care. My sons and I did make the time to be together, and I have few regrets there. I just wish that I had been more disciplined and thorough in giving them the kind of advice every father should make sure his sons receive before they move out from under his roof.

These topics are some of the things we talked about, some of the things I wished we had talked about, and some of the things I did not even realize they needed to know until events in their lives brought them to the surface.

Have a great time with your sons! May the younger ones be so envious of their older brothers that they cannot wait for their turn with Dad—even if it is just to go through some old book. Keep the momentum going!

Make the most of these days, gentlemen!

HOW TO USE THIS BOOK

It is my hope that you can use these brief thoughts as a springboard to compile your own list of fatherly advice to give to your guys "just one more thing" before they go. Solomon put together quite an extensive series of thoughts in the book of Proverbs. Consider these bits of advice and counsel as one Dad's "proverbs" for his sons before they launch out into life on their own. The greatest contribution I see in offering this compilation to you is that you can go over these topics with your own sons and talk about them together each week. Here is what I would suggest you try.

1. When your son reaches 14 or 15, you probably will wonder what happened to the little guy who couldn't get enough of your time. Now, at this age, you probably are hard-pressed to get him to talk much at all. With that in mind, I reduced my growing list to 52 bits and pieces of advice. Sometime around your son's freshman or sophomore year in high school, I suggest that you take one son at a time all the way through the book, discussing one thought per week for a year.

2. If you can set aside a scheduled time of 10 to 15 minutes on a Sunday night before your week gets into full swing (or some other night that works better with your own schedule), you will in all likelihood be spending 10 to 15 times more quality time than you were before. The value will not necessarily be in the content of the material you are going over as much as the fact that you and your adolescent son are actually talking about something of substance each week.

3. You know your son better than I do, but if he is like my guys were in the ninth or tenth grade, the last thing he will want to do is have a face-to-face, sit-down discussion with good old Dad! Therefore, it is important to let him know that you will probably be able to cover the basics in a little more than 10 minutes with a few minutes left for small talk. Keep it brief and to the point during the first few weeks, and you will meet less resistance as the year goes on.

4. Remember, what you and I consider fun will not appear to be so to him. Be patient and do not get your hopes up about having him nominate you for the "Father of the Year Award" for successful Christian parenting!

5. Just one more thing before you get started—make sure that you spend a part of each session praying together.

> W hatever you do, in word or in deed, do it as unto the Lord. Give it everything you've got as you pursue excellence for Christ.

Whatever you do, in word or deed, do all in the name of the Lord Jesus, giving thanks through Him to God the Father ... Whatever you do, do your work heartily, as for the Lord rather than for men ...
Colossians 3:17, 23

We are *called* to excellence by Christ, not driven to it by compulsive urges or perfectionist tendencies. Purify the motive and then when it is all for Christ, go *flat out!* Commit yourself to the discipline and hard work necessary to maximize the gifts and talents God has given you.

Never settle for less than your very best. Even if you have natural abilities that set you apart from your peers, resist the temptation to "make do" with these abilities in their unrefined state. Instead, determine to build and develop them so that you "excel still more" as the Apostle Paul says in 1 Thessalonians 4:1. Paul also tells young Timothy to fan his gifts into flame, making the most of what he received from the Lord (2 Timothy 1:6). How can we be satisfied in doing anything less?

Just one more thing . . .

Pick an area in which you are only giving a half-hearted effort. What do you need to do to give it everything you've got? What difference would this make in the amount of glory God gets and how much satisfaction you get?

_____

_____

_____

_____

_____

_____

_____

_____

_____

_____

_____

Learn to take Jesus and others *more* seriously and yourself *less* seriously.

For through the grace given to me I say to every man among you not to think more highly of himself than he ought to think; but to think so as to have sound judgment, as God has allotted to each a measure of faith.   Romans 12:3

All of us have a tendency to be overly serious about what we think, feel, and want. We often do not take into account what matters to others. The difference between what really matters and what we think matters will often define when we should take things more seriously and when we should lighten up!

Although what you think and feel about things is important to you, this does not guarantee that you are right or that others have an obligation to adjust their perspectives to match yours. Allow for the possibility that you could be attaching far more importance to the matter at hand than is really necessary.

Just one more thing . . .

Do you remember a time when you were
embarrassed by the way you responded to a
situation or person? How would it have been
different if you had attached a lot less importance to
what you wanted and more to what Jesus wanted?

_____

_____

_____

_____

_____

_____

_____

_____

_____

_____

> **C**hoose your friends with great care, asking the Lord to give you friends who will bring out the best in you and the Christlike qualities most suited to glorifying God.

A friend loves at all times, and a brother is born for adversity. Proverbs 17:17

And if one can overpower him who is alone, two can resist him. A cord of three strands is not quickly torn apart. Ecclesiastes 4:12

Some friends are fun to be with but exact a great toll on your spiritual interests and development. Every godly man needs to have biblically sound friendships with those who have earned the right to ask hard questions, to hold him accountable, and to challenge him to walk humbly and with integrity before God.

One day your wife should be your best friend. But don't miss the value of having a couple of "soul mates" now who know you, who know Christ, and who long to know both better. Always be looking for those special relationships that can be lifelong commitments to pray for each other and encourage each other in the Lord.

Just one more thing...

If you do not currently have friends who bring out the best of Christ in you, how can you go about finding them? And if you already have these friends, how do you intend to keep them?

Develop the ability to laugh at yourself and be slow to take offense when others laugh at you or your mistakes.

Patience of spirit is better than haughtiness of spirit. Do not be eager in your heart to be angry, for anger resides in the bosom of fools. Ecclesiastes 7:8–9

He who is slow to anger has great understanding, but he who is quick-tempered exalts folly. Proverbs 14:29

Usually our first reaction is to take offense when others laugh at us, which is entirely normal because we are embarrassed. Yet if we take a moment to look at what we have done or at the circumstances that prompted their response, we too might find the humor if we can step back and look at things objectively.

If you cannot laugh at yourself, you will develop an attitude of superiority that suggests that you are above making normal mistakes and routine "goof-ups." No one likes to be around folks with that attitude! Therefore, learn to resist the impulse to take offense and in genuine humility try to see things from the perspective of the person who has offended you.

Just one more thing . . .

Remember the last time you became upset when
someone laughed at you? What would have
happened if instead of being offended and
embarrassed, you had just realized the humor
in the situation and joined in the laughter?

_____

_____

_____

_____

_____

_____

_____

_____

_____

_____

_____

Never claim for yourself the right to center stage or behave in such a way that you dominate other people by the force of your personality.

When you are invited by someone to a wedding feast, do not take the place of honor, lest someone more distinguished than you may have been invited by him, and he who invited you both shall come and say to you, "Give place to this man," and then in disgrace you proceed to occupy the last place . . . For everyone who exalts himself shall be humbled, and he who humbles himself shall be exalted.   Luke 14:8–9, 11

Be careful not to speak too boisterously or loudly in public. When you do, it looks like you are trying unwisely to draw attention to yourself. In fact, you will invite more pity than affirmation if you behave this way because others may think you are insecure or are trying to satisfy a need to be noticed. On the other hand, if you do so because you think more highly of yourself than you ought, your behavior will send a message that your ego is too big, and people will do their best to avoid you.

Whether you draw unnecessary attention to yourself from insecurity or because of self-absorption, the bottom line is that you need to become more content to step back out of the spotlight. Let others bring you to the front instead of forcing yourself into that position.

16

Just one more thing . . .

Get a good friend to help you catch yourself
when you are getting too loud, too forceful, or too
overpowering when you are with a group. Then
be prepared to back down graciously and humbly.

_____

_____

_____

_____

_____

_____

_____

_____

_____

_____

_____

_____

Work as hard as you must to develop the habit and practice of prayer. Devote a period of time every day to talk with the Lord and then listen quietly to hear His voice.

Devote yourselves to prayer, keeping alert in it with an attitude of thanksgiving.   Colossians 4:2

Pray without ceasing.   1 Thessalonians 5:17

The most difficult thing I do is pray since it is not a natural or comfortable matter for me, even though I know the importance of growing a mature and dynamic prayer life. Bad habits are hard to break, and good habits are hard to develop. Prayerlessness is a habit that must be broken and prayerfulness a habit that must be developed.

Although the possibility of becoming legalistic does exist in prayer, it is much easier to steer a moving vehicle than a parked one. Therefore, set an established minimum for daily prayer time or else you will find that you will always be "intending to pray" or feeling badly that you neglected to pray. Above all, do not study prayer, talk about prayer, read about prayer, and then never actually get around to praying!

Just one more thing . . .

Choose a time and a place and then get started today in building a habit of praying every day.

_____

_____

_____

_____

_____

_____

_____

_____

_____

_____

_____

_____

_____

Maintain a sane estimation of who you are and what you can do, striving to keep a humble attitude about yourself.

But He gives a greater grace. Therefore it says, "God is opposed to the proud, but gives grace to the humble." ... Humble yourselves in the presence of the Lord, and He will exalt you. James 4:6,10

Always take the greatest precaution against speaking of yourself in a way that might be misunderstood as boasting or demonstrating an elevated opinion of yourself. Generally speaking, people do not like to be around braggarts who seem to have no end of stories about themselves.

A simple formula I learned as a child has always provided an excellent measure to check my attitude. To keep a sane estimation of yourself, make sure that your focus is on . . .

> Jesus, then
> Others, and then
> You!

Jesus, others, and you—what a wonderful way not only to spell JOY but to experience it!

Just one more thing . . .

Be sure to think twice the next time you find
yourself starting to brag about yourself.
Remember to take the low place for yourself
and give the high place to Jesus and to others.

_____

_____

_____

_____

_____

_____

_____

_____

_____

_____

_____

_____

Always give people the benefit of the doubt when they do something you do not like or something that hurts you.

[Love] is not rude, it is not self-seeking, it is not easily angered, it keeps no record of wrongs.
1 Corinthians 13:5 (NIV)

Through carelessness or simple inconsideration, people wound one another regularly. Instead of assigning evil motives and malicious intent to their actions or words, give them the benefit of the doubt and assume that they meant no harm. Otherwise, you may get angry and hold grudges against people who never intended to hurt you. If you assume the worst about people and constantly question their motives, you will have a hard time getting over the idea that everyone is out to get you! In many cases, their intentions were not malicious. Be fair with them before you jump to the wrong conclusion. You will find that you are a happier person and have far less enemies.

Just one more thing . . .

Ask yourself if there are people you can think of
who seem to be doing or saying things as if they
were out to get you. Giving them the benefit of the
doubt, is it possible that they never intended to
hurt your feelings? Have you assumed things
about them that may not really be true?

_____

_____

_____

_____

_____

_____

_____

_____

_____

_____

> **A**lways be aware that wherever you go and whatever you do, someone is watching and making note of your behavior and attitude.

Behold, you have sinned against the LORD, and be sure your sin will find you out.   Numbers 32:23

Your actions always come back to you in a way you never expect. A city beat news reporter in Boston once told me that there are people who make a living keeping their eyes open for behavior that can be exploited for monetary gain. They hang out near places where immoral and illegal activities take place, writing down license plate numbers of cars and taking pictures of people as they come and go. Then they find ways to use that information to blackmail public figures or anyone else who might be willing to pay not to have their sin exposed. The moral of the reporter's story was brutally clear—never put yourself in a position to do something you would not want broadcast on the evening news!

Even in private places or when you think no one notices, someone does, *always!* Whether it is looking at a magazine in an airport newsstand or watching inappropriate movies in hotel rooms when you are away from home, someone takes note. You can never be sure who that someone may be or what that person might do with the information. Obviously the best deterrent to such impure behavior is recognizing that you are the temple of the Holy Spirit. Nothing should ever be introduced to your body or mind that would soil the holiness of His dwelling place. It also helps to remember that when you least expect it, you might be watched by someone who would love to "bring you down" as a Christian and destroy your testimony and reputation.

Such knowledge alone should prevent you from indulging in some secret sin when you are tempted to drop your guard. It is a strong deterrent knowing that although you think no one you know is around, someone is taking note!

Just one more thing . . .

Before you decide to go where you shouldn't go, see what you shouldn't see, or do what you shouldn't do, ask yourself this: Would you do it if you knew someone was watching? Jesus always is!

_____

_____

_____

_____

_____

_____

_____

_____

Order your life according to an intentional, principled set of biblical priorities. They will keep you from living a frantic and busy life without any sense of spiritual fulfillment.

But seek first His kingdom and His righteousness; and all these things shall be added to you.   Matthew 6:33

But the Lord answered and said to her, "Martha, Martha, you are worried and bothered about so many things; but only a few things are necessary, really only one, for Mary has chosen the good part, which shall not be taken away from her."   Luke 10:41–42

Busy is not necessarily better. Resist, therefore, the temptation to fill your life and the life of your family with too many things to do. When you are too busy, you cannot keep the pace of your hectic schedule without violating the integrity of your priorities to live and to do all things for the glory of Christ.

Many have missed the quiet direction of the Lord because they could not be still long enough to hear Him. Make time to be still and listen to God. Take time to read, reflect, and meditate on the Word. It's also important to relax and allow your body, soul, and spirit to be refreshed through godly rest.

Just one more thing . . .

Make a short list of your top priorities and
compare them with what currently occupies most
of your time and energy at this point in your life.

_____

_____

_____

_____

_____

_____

_____

_____

_____

_____

_____

_____

_____

Make up your mind to never allow yourself to have an enemy, regardless of those who choose to make an enemy of you.

If therefore you are presenting your offering at the altar, and there remember that your brother has something against you, leave your offering there before the altar, and go your way; first be reconciled to your brother, and then come and present your offering. Matthew 5:23–24

If possible, so far as it depends on you, be at peace with all men.   Romans 12:18

While you cannot control how others respond to you, you can control how you respond to them, doing everything in your power to be a peacemaker. If they refuse to be reconciled with you, then in your heart and mind make sure that you do not indulge your anger, bitterness, or secret desire for revenge.

Always be on the lookout for ways to offer kindness, not meanness, to these people. Speak of them in your prayers, not in slanderous conversations, and work toward restoration of the relationship, refusing to allow any root of bitterness to get hold of you.

Acting from revenge or spite is never an acceptable option! As far as it depends on you, be at peace with everyone, even those who want to consider you as their enemy.

Just one more thing . . .

Ask yourself if there is anyone in your life right now to whom you need to be reconciled. How do you plan to go about restoring your relationship?

_____

_____

_____

_____

_____

_____

_____

_____

_____

_____

_____

_____

_____

Resist the pressure of our culture to relate to others based on the color of their skin or the socioeconomic conditions from which they come.

... There is no distinction between Greek and Jew, circumcised and uncircumcised, barbarian, Scythian, slave and freeman, but Christ is all, and in all. Colossians 3:11

My brethren, do not hold your faith in our glorious Lord Jesus Christ with an attitude of personal favoritism. For if a man comes into your assembly with a gold ring and dressed in fine clothes, and there also comes in a poor man in dirty clothes, and you pay special attention to the one who is wearing the fine clothes, and say, "You sit here in a good place," and you say to the poor man, "You stand over there, or sit down by my footstool," have you not made distinctions among yourselves, and become judges with evil motives? James 2:1–4

Racism is an insidious evil that invades our thinking in subtle ways. It creates within us a bias or prejudice that prevents us from relating to people as unique individuals created in the image of God. Determine early in your life that *you* will take the initiative to develop relationships with people who are different from you. If you do, stereotypes will soon be exposed as unsubstantiated and discrimination will become intolerable when viewed in the context of meaningful relationships.

Even though everyone notices personal differences, the key to avoiding partiality is to refuse to be adversely influenced by those differences. You can then overcome the racial, ethnic, cultural, and socioeconomic distinctions that get in the way of forming sound friendships.

Just one more thing . . .

Take the initiative to develop an ongoing relationship with someone who is from a different background from your own. When and where and with whom will you get started?

_____

_____

_____

_____

_____

_____

_____

Always remember the awesome power of your words, both for good and for evil.

But no one can tame the tongue; it is a restless evil and full of deadly poison. With it we bless our Lord and Father; and with it we curse men, who have been made in the likeness of God; from the same mouth come both blessing and cursing. My brethren, these things ought not to be this way.   James 3:8–10

Let no unwholesome word proceed from your mouth, but only such a word as is good for edification according to the need of the moment, that it may give grace to those who hear.   Ephesians 4:29

What you say, and often *how* you say it, can bring terrible destruction to yourself and others, or it can build up and encourage. Be careful to guard your tongue and choose your words wisely.

Gossip and slander are malicious tools. Determine to refrain from both and avoid people who make a habit of them. Make up your mind that if you speak of someone else it will be a profitable comment. Even if you have a legitimate criticism, you can express it with an attitude that builds up and does not tear down.

When you speak ill of others, it nearly always either gets back to them or affects the way you relate to them since you know you have wronged them.

Just one more thing...

Examine your words and motives before you talk about someone or to someone. If you cannot speak in a way that builds them up rather than tears them down, say nothing at all!

Congratulations!

You've just completed the first lap! If you've ever seen a track meet, then you may know that the mile run is made up of four laps of 440 yards. Since there are 52 weeks in a year, there are 52 proverbs so that you can shoot for the goal of covering one per week.

You have just finished 13—one-fourth of the way! Why not take some time to celebrate together? Go out and get something to eat together as a way to mark the completion of the first lap.

Frankly, it may have taken you much longer than 13 weeks to get this far. So? You're not competing with anyone. You just want to keep plodding away until you finish the race!

Be encouraged and keep on going.

Learn the joy of leading others by serving them, not lifting yourself up by putting them down.

Shepherd the flock of God among you, exercising oversight not under compulsion, but voluntarily, according to the will of God; and not for sordid gain, but with eagerness; nor yet as lording it over those allotted to your charge, but proving to be examples to the flock.   1 Peter 5:2–3

Sometimes people respond to leaders who push them around, to those who are demanding and self-serving. But more often, people are drawn to servant-leaders, those who demonstrate a willingness to work alongside and not stand at a distance shouting orders. A servant-leader *wins* respect instead of *demanding* it.

Should you find yourself in a position of leadership, you will find that you will be most effective when you are willing to put others first. When they realize that you care about them as well as where you are leading them, they will gladly follow you.

Just one more thing . . .

Start preparing to be a godly leader by finding a place to serve now and learn how to be a servant. Only in serving will you ever be equipped to lead God's way.

_____

_____

_____

_____

_____

_____

_____

_____

_____

_____

_____

_____

Learn how to have a meaningful quiet time every day that includes not only a time for prayer, but also invests profitable time studying God's Word.

Be diligent to present yourself approved to God as a workman who does not need to be ashamed, handling accurately the word of truth.   2 Timothy 2:15

Thy word I have treasured in my heart, that I may not sin against Thee.   Psalm 119:11

Devotional books and study guides are wonderful tools and great aids to understanding the Bible, but they cannot become a substitute for "hands-on" interaction with the Scriptures.

Maintain a current Bible reading and study plan that allows you to work through the Scriptures in a thorough and systematic manner over prescribed periods of time. In order to keep yourself from letting your routine get boring, mix things up once in a while so that your reading and study do not become mechanical or predictable. Make sure you leave some time for thinking about what you've read and asking the Lord how it applies to your life.

Just one more thing . . .

Decide to keep your appointment with the Lord every day and work on a proper balance between the time you spend in prayer and the time you spend reading and studying the Bible.

_____

_____

_____

_____

_____

_____

_____

_____

_____

_____

_____

_____

Take time on a regular basis to be alone so that you can think, reflect, meditate, dream, and plan in pursuing a clear vision for your life.

This book of the law shall not depart from your mouth, but you shall meditate on it day and night, so that you may be careful to do according to all that is written in it; for then you will make your way prosperous, and then you will have success.   Joshua 1:8

Where there is no vision, the people are unrestrained, but happy is he who keeps the law.   Proverbs 29:18

Without a plan or vision for your life, you cannot live with the kind of purpose and passion that God intended.

Learn how to plan, look ahead, anticipate potential problems, propose and pursue probable solutions, and organize an orderly process to achieve your objective.

Think ahead, gather your facts, and check the accuracy of your assumptions. Carpenters have an excellent saying: "Measure twice, cut once." Rushing ahead just to get something done proves to be rewarded usually with inferior results or most often the need to start over. Therefore, think ahead and do it right the first time and be patient if it takes longer than you think.

Just one more thing . . .

Schedule a couple of hours this week to dream a little and ask yourself what you would like to be doing five to ten years from now. What do you think you would need to start doing now to move in that direction?

_____

_____

_____

_____

_____

_____

_____

_____

_____

_____

_____

_____

Learn the value of deferred gratification with respect to financial commitment and resist the temptation to make purchases on impulse.

Rest in the LORD and wait patiently for Him; do not fret because of him who prospers in his way, because of the man who carries out wicked schemes . . . Wait for the LORD, and keep His way, and He will exalt you to inherit the land; when the wicked are cut off, you will see it. Psalm 37:7, 34

Do not talk yourself into thinking that whatever you want, you need to get it "right now." Deferred gratification means that you wait until a more suitable time to get what you want. Impulsive spending often leads to financial instability and misses the satisfaction of planning ahead, setting goals, and reaching them. Never trivialize the sense of accomplishment you will enjoy by learning to be patient and wait. Learn to make your purchases according to wise planning and comparison shopping. It is true—good things come to those who wait.

Just one more thing . . .

Practice patience by saying "no" to yourself about something you really want right now but know that it would really be better if you waited.

_____

_____

_____

_____

_____

_____

_____

_____

_____

_____

_____

_____

Never give up. Keep going through the tape at the finish; run through the bag at first base.

Do you not know that those who run in a race all run, but only one receives the prize? Run in such a way that you may win.   1 Corinthians 9:24

I press on toward the goal for the prize of the upward call of God in Christ Jesus.   Philippians 3:14

The difference between those who prosper and succeed and those who muddle through life is often found in how they finish what they are doing. Too many settle for a good start and good intentions but never carry through their plans to completion. When you start something, give it your best shot all the way through to the end. If the race is tougher than you thought or longer than you imagined, don't be a quitter!

Discouragement can make you want to settle for less, and people will often advise you to give in and give up. But if what you are doing has meaning and value, do not be satisfied with anything less than finishing what you have begun and finishing *well.*

Just one more thing . . .

Something you are facing right now may not be
going the way you had hoped, and you may be
seriously considering giving up instead of going at
it with all you've got. Go on and finish well what
you started!

Maintain an up-to-date list of people who need to know Christ as Savior and pray for them.

The Lord is not slow about His promise, as some count slowness, but is patient toward you, not wishing for any to perish but for all to come to repentance.
2 Peter 3:9

An evangelistic prayer list serves as a daily reminder not only to pray for those who are searching for Christ, but to remain alert to opportunities to make known the love of Christ to them (first in what you do, then in what you say). Keep this list with your quiet time materials or carry it in your Bible or your wallet so that you will be diligent to pray for them each day.

It is too easy to neglect the calling of Christ to be His witnesses. Often we end up never sharing the gospel with anyone because it is not a priority or a commitment either in prayer or in practice. If we are convinced that Christ is the Way, the Truth, and the Life and no one comes to the Father but through Him, we cannot sit by doing nothing while those around us never know of His great love for them.

Just one more thing . . .

Write down the names of several people you would love to see come to know Christ and then start praying for them consistently.

B e careful not to associate with those who tend to act irresponsibly, either out of anger, immaturity, lack of respect for others, or in general disregard for appropriate behavior.

Do not associate with a man given to anger; or go with a hot-tempered man, lest you learn his ways, and find a snare for yourself.   Proverbs 22:24–25

Most of us have seen what happens when someone we know gets out of hand. If you hang around with such people, your resistance will gradually be lowered. They will soon influence you to follow their pattern of destructive behavior. Beyond the simple embarrassment of seeing them make fools of themselves, you also put yourself in a position of being drawn into their foolishness and doing something you would normally never do. Making a habit of hanging out with people who constantly get out of control is simply begging for trouble.

Just one more thing . . .

Think about which friends and acquaintances have a tendency to get out of control and into trouble regularly. Take steps to distance yourself from them and their irresponsible behavior.

> **T**reasure the special women God places in your life and never compromise their purity or their holiness.

Do not sharply rebuke an older man, but rather appeal to him as a father, to the younger men as brothers, the older women as mothers, and the younger women as sisters, in all purity.   1 Timothy 5:1–2

Let no one look down on your youthfulness, but rather in speech, conduct, love, faith and purity, show yourself an example of those who believe.
1 Timothy 4:12

In your younger years, those "special women" may be your mother, grandmothers, teachers, girlfriends, or other women who are important to you. Treat each of them as a treasure, someone of great value. When you marry, you will want to treat your wife as that most special woman of all in your life, with honor. Developing healthy habits and learning how to relate to women in a godly manner *now* will provide a mature, growing context for your future relationship with your wife.

Sometimes guys lose sight of their own insensitivities and lack of discernment when they are around women. Men can actually treat women in ways detrimental to their spiritual growth by making crass and demeaning comments, using unsavory humor, and by choosing impure entertainment and recreational activities. This is not to suggest that women have no choices of their own, but just a word of caution to not place stumbling blocks in their way.

Just one more thing...

Determine now before you start spending regular time with a young woman that you will never do anything or be anywhere that would have a detrimental impact on her growth in godliness.

_____

_____

_____

_____

_____

_____

_____

_____

_____

_____

_____

Recognize your lifelong need to be an active, functional member of a local congregation.

Let us consider how to stimulate one another to love and good deeds, not forsaking our own assembling together, as is the habit of some, but encouraging one another; and all the more, as you see the day drawing near.   Hebrews 10:24–25

God has called each of us into the body of Christ as joint participants with one another. When you are an active part of a local congregation, you can experience celebrative worship in a large group context and accountable relationships in a small group context. In this way, we can be built up to maturity together, benefiting from the unique contributions each of us make to our mutual growth. If you neglect corporate worship, you lose touch with the majesty and glory of God of which we are reminded when in the presence of others praising and adoring the Lord. If you neglect the small group relationships that develop spiritual intimacy and accountability, you risk a detached, disinterested, and "arms length" faith that is both sterile and unsatisfying.

Make sure that you get involved personally and practically in large and small group ministry situations where Christ is the focus and God's Word is the foundation.

Just one more thing . . .

Ask yourself what you are doing now to instill the godly habit of actively engaging in the ministry life of a local congregation. What can you do to get ready for the day you are on your own and need to find a church home?

_____

_____

_____

_____

_____

_____

_____

_____

_____

_____

A s you come across people who are very easy to dislike, cultivate the habit of speaking a kind word to them and looking for ways to be gracious to them.

But if your enemy is hungry, feed him, and if he is thirsty, give him a drink; for in so doing you will heap burning coals upon his head. Do not be overcome by evil, but overcome evil with good.   Romans 12:20–21

Y ou can always justify your reasons for not liking thoroughly disagreeable people. You can possibly even make a case for treating them the way you think they deserve. But as God's chosen agent of reconciliation and witness to Christ's love, rise above your feelings and respond to them with grace, dignity, and kindness. Although they might not always respond the way you would like, when you treat people the way you would like to be treated, you are more likely to overcome evil with good.

Don't expect them to be overly impressed by your kindness. They probably will never say anything and may not even notice. Still, you will know that you have modeled the love of Christ in what you did.

Just one more thing . . .

Is there someone in your life right now who tests your resolve to be kind? What can you do to show this person the genuine love of Christ?

_____

_____

_____

_____

_____

_____

_____

_____

_____

_____

_____

_____

_____

Model generosity in your way
of life as an expression of the giving
nature of the Lord and as a counter-
balance to the materialism so
rampant in our culture.

For you know the grace of our Lord Jesus Christ, that
though He was rich, yet for your sake He became poor,
that you through His poverty might become rich.
2 Corinthians 8:9

Whenever possible, find ways to encourage that generous
spirit by looking for ways to give to meet the needs of others,
but not only with your money. Look for opportunities to
volunteer to work in ministry situations with the poor and
needy to keep the right perspective of the rich blessings God
has poured out on you. Remember how generous the Lord
has been to you and make up your mind to find a way to do
the same thing for others. If you stop to think how generous
God has been to you, you will find it easier to be more
generous to others.

Just one more thing...

Recognizing the abundance with which God has
blessed you, find a place or a person with needs
and out of your own resources give generously
toward meeting those needs.

_____

_____

_____

_____

_____

_____

_____

_____

_____

_____

_____

_____

Avoid situations where alcohol and drugs will probably be in use so that you will not place yourself in jeopardy either by association, by victimization, or by temptation.

Do not enter the path of the wicked, and do not proceed in the way of evil men. Avoid it, do not pass by it; turn away from it and pass on.   Proverbs 4:14–15

Now flee from youthful lusts, and pursue righteousness, faith, love and peace, with those who call on the Lord from a pure heart.   2 Timothy 2:22

In my life I have known too many who have fallen into one of those three problems—guilt by association, victimization by those under the influence, or temptation to join the crowd. Frequently associating with people who use alcohol or drugs will lead others to assume that you are involved in the same activity. I have seen innocent individuals victimized by either serious injury or death because they were with people who had gotten out of control. Temptation is also a major problem because it is extremely difficult to stand firm when so many others have chosen to do otherwise.

The scriptural solution is simple: Flee from such things! Don't put yourself in a situation with such potentially serious consequences.

Just one more thing . . .

Before a situation with alcohol or drugs ever comes up, decide well in advance what you will do so that you are not forced to react on the spur of the moment instead of being prepared to act wisely.

Should it become necessary to criticize, challenge, or confront someone, exercise wise caution but do not shy away from doing what must be done.

Brethren, even if a man is caught in any trespass, you who are spiritual, restore such a one in a spirit of gentleness; each one looking to yourself, lest you too be tempted.   Galatians 6:1

Before you criticize, challenge, or confront someone, make sure that 1) you are the proper one to do so; 2) the issue really needs to be addressed and is not a matter of personal opinion or preference; 3) you have checked your own motives and attitude; and 4) you have prayed for the right words, right circumstances (in private if at all possible), and right purpose (the glory of Christ and the good of the person).

In the long run, it is more loving to speak up than to shut up when you see someone heading in the wrong direction. They may not initially appreciate what you have to say, but Proverbs 28:23 says, "He who rebukes a man will afterward find more favor than he who flatters with the tongue."

Just one more thing . . .

Think back to a situation in which you should
have spoken up to help a friend avoid trouble, but
you chose not to do so. What are some good ways
to approach a friend if you find that you have a
difficult message to communicate?

_____

_____

_____

_____

_____

_____

_____

_____

_____

_____

Halfway there!

Time to celebrate again. Another lap is behind you and only two more to go. I have an idea some of you never thought your son or dad would make it this far, but here you are!

Runners talk about hitting a wall when they run a long distance race. About now in your year together, you may be tempted to let up—maybe even to give up. That's why there are two of you together, each one to encourage the other to stay on course.

Plan a special treat to celebrate this time. Maybe a ballgame or an overnight event if you want to go all out. Or just a nice dinner or dessert for the two of you.

A lot of dads and sons have never done what you are doing, so give thanks to the Lord for each other when you pray together today.

Encourage each other to stay on course.

Strive for simplicity in your life by resisting the natural tendency to add layers of complexity that will distract you from a life of simple trust in Christ.

And she had a sister called Mary, who moreover was listening to the Lord's word, seated at His feet. But Martha was distracted with all her preparations; and she came up to Him, and said, "Lord, do You not care that my sister has left me to do all the serving alone? Then tell her to help me." But the Lord answered and said to her, "Martha, Martha, you are worried and bothered about so many things; but only a few things are necessary, really only one, for Mary has chosen the good part, which shall not be taken away from her." Luke 10:39–42

When you complicate your life with so many things that demand your attention and energy, you endanger your spiritual growth. You will make it more difficult on yourself to maintain quality times of listening to the Lord, learning of His direction and how simple life can be when we find Him to be all-sufficient. If God is all that matters, you will find how little you really need everything else that constantly works to complicate your life. Sometimes even good things can get in the way of the best things. Periodically take some time to clear out all the clutter that complicates your life and focus on what is best.

Just one more thing . . .

Identify some of the things going on in your life that are keeping you very busy. In the eternal purposes of God, should these things be real priorities for you? What would happen if you eliminated them?

When bad things happen in your life, choose to respond with the grace and dignity of Christ rather than reacting in a way that will cause you to be ashamed later.

Yet I will exult in the Lord, I will rejoice in the God of my salvation. The Lord God is my strength, and He has made my feet like hinds' feet, and makes me walk on my high places. *Habakkuk 3:18–19*

How you respond to difficulties is a choice, one that can be made with wisdom, discernment, and self-control or out of anger, foolishness, and frustration. Choose wisely in the little frustrations so that you are trained properly when bad things happen on a much larger scale.

When you feel like life is crashing in all around you, look to the Lord for strength and understanding. Through Christ, you can hold your head up and carry on because you know that ultimately He will do what is best for you.

Just one more thing . . .

Do you recall a time when you allowed yourself to get out of control, a reaction that embarrasses you now as you remember what you did? Should a similar situation arise again, what kind of response would honor Christ more?

_____

_____

_____

_____

_____

_____

_____

_____

_____

_____

_____

Develop a lifelong pattern of being a mentor to others as well as finding mentors for yourself.

And the things which you have heard from me in the presence of many witnesses, these entrust to faithful men, who will be able to teach others also.
2 Timothy 2:2

If you succeed in any endeavor, there will always be someone who would benefit greatly from your experience and appreciate your taking a personal, special interest in him. Be careful not to be so consumed with your own agenda that you ignore others who could really use your help.

Likewise, wherever you are heading with your life, there are others who have gone along the same course before you. Look for people with the same godly values and vision. They would prove to be invaluable mentors for you as you seek God's best for your life.

Just one more thing . . .

Look for people who could be good role models for you and find out if they would be willing to invest a little of themselves in you. At the same time, make sure that you are open to do the same for someone else.

_____

_____

_____

_____

_____

_____

_____

_____

_____

_____

_____

Learn how to ask questions of others to find out more about them, rather than trying to find ways to direct attention to yourself.

Do nothing from selfishness or empty conceit, but with humility of mind let each of you regard one another as more important than himself; do not merely look out for your own personal interests, but also for the interests of others. Philippians 2:3–4

When there are many words, transgression is unavoidable, but he who restrains his lips is wise. Proverbs 10:19

The natural tendency in all of us is to enjoy talking about ourselves, so it is important whenever possible to turn that around and honor other people by asking about them. Rather than multiplying our own words, we should restrain ourselves from talking and learn to listen instead. Genuine interest in others honors them. Listening rather than talking bestows that honor.

By giving it a little thought, you can easily come up with a few, well-designed questions that you are comfortable asking others. Learn to draw others out and communicate to them that you care about them. It will also force you to focus more attention on them and less attention on yourself.

Just one more thing...

Take note of how much of your conversation centers on what you have to say rather than showing that you care about others. Intentionally ask questions that will shift the focus to others, rather than to yourself.

_____

_____

_____

_____

_____

_____

_____

_____

_____

_____

_____

Operate your finances within a well-defined budget so that the priorities of your life will be demonstrated by sound, disciplined spending practices.

"Bring the whole tithe into the storehouse, so that there may be food in My house, and test Me now in this," says the LORD of hosts, "if I will not open for you the windows of heaven, and pour out for you a blessing until it overflows."   Malachi 3:10

For the love of money is a root of all sorts of evil, and some by longing for it have wandered away from the faith, and pierced themselves with many a pang. 1 Timothy 6:10

The starting point for building a budget must be the amount of available funds *after* tithes and offerings have been set apart for the Lord. Otherwise, you are tempted to move God's portion from first place to last place and tithe only if there is something left!

Begin now to learn how to live within your means. Someday, after you marry, resist the temptation to establish a standard of living that requires two incomes (from both you and your wife) to sustain. Choose to live on just one income when possible and do not be enticed into a financial commitment that assumes both of you must work. The result will be a life of faith ordered on godly priorities and free from the pain of longing and worrying about money.

Just one more thing...

Take a look at your spending habits to make sure that you have obeyed the Lord with your tithes and offerings. Also check to see that the balance of your spending is consistent with the biblical priorities you uphold.

_____

_____

_____

_____

_____

_____

_____

_____

_____

_____

_____

Whenever you are in a public place, notice the way men look at women and determine in your heart and mind never to treat women that way. Never think of them as mere objects to be leered at or lusted over.

"You have heard that it was said, 'You shall not commit adultery'; but I say to you, that everyone who looks on a woman to lust for her has committed adultery with her already in his heart."
Matthew 5:27–28

If you become aware of how awful this habit is by observing it in others, you can avoid repeating it yourself. Choose instead to develop a much healthier approach toward members of the opposite sex. Beyond the obvious disrespect for the woman who is the focus of such inappropriate attention, the temptation to entertain lustful thoughts makes it also a matter of moral and spiritual concern for yourself. Therefore, be careful with your eyes and with your attitude in the way you treat women.

Just one more thing . . .

Discipline your heart and mind to see women as
God does—individuals who have great value in
His eyes. Never allow yourself to forget that God
created women and yourself for purity.

Learn how to accept a compliment graciously but without taking the credit.

You younger men, likewise, be subject to your elders; and all of you, clothe yourselves with humility toward one another, for God is opposed to the proud, but gives grace to the humble.   1 Peter 5:5

The crucible for silver and the furnace for gold, but man is tested by the praise he receives. (NIV) Proverbs 27:21

Two extremes often occur when people are complimented. Either they accept the compliment believing they deserve it, or they reject it believing they should act more humbly by deflecting compliments. Rather than acting according to either extreme, the proper way to accept the compliment is simply to say, "Thank you. You are very kind (or very gracious)." Then as soon as you have said these words with your lips, offer the compliment with your heart to the Lord and give Him both the glory and the credit.

Do not turn the compliment away by saying, "Oh, that's not me but the Lord!" You may say this with good motives, but it often makes others feel very awkward as if they should have thought of that themselves or are not as "spiritually sensitive" as you.

Just one more thing . . .

Next time someone compliments you, receive it graciously, but then pass it right along to the Lord without keeping any part of it for yourself.

_____

_____

_____

_____

_____

_____

_____

_____

_____

_____

_____

_____

Guard your words carefully around acquaintances who delight in passing on gossip and stirring up strife.

For lack of wood the fire goes out, and where there is no whisperer, contention quiets down. Like charcoal to hot embers and wood to fire, so is a contentious man to kindle strife. The words of a whisperer are like dainty morsels, and they go down into the innermost parts of the body.   Proverbs 26:20–22

*He who goes about as a slanderer reveals secrets, therefore do not associate with a gossip.
Proverbs 20:19*

Like a bad tooth and an unsteady foot is confidence in a faithless man in time of trouble.   Proverbs 25:19

Exercise good judgment in selecting those with whom you share confidential information lest it come back on you with a vengeance! Many friendships have been destroyed because of indiscreet talk and breaches of trust between those who assumed a higher level of trust than actually existed.

Be a person who can keep confidences, and you will always be considered a trustworthy and faithful friend. If you do not own the information yourself, do not give away what does not belong to you.

Just one more thing...

This week, before you pass on any information that you would be embarrassed to hear repeated and attributed to you, ask yourself the following:

1) Why do you want to tell it?
2) Is the person you are speaking with trustworthy?
3) Do you really want to run the risk of passing on hurtful information?
4) Would you be embarrassed if the source was traced back to you?

> When you make a mistake, injure someone, or in any way create a problem for someone, offer your sincere apology as soon as you realize your fault.

Be kind to one another, tender-hearted, forgiving each other, just as God in Christ also has forgiven you.
Ephesians 4:32

Saying "I'm sorry" or "I was wrong" goes a long way in building character in you and respect for you from others. No one expects to be right or do right 100 percent of the time, so it is refreshing to others to hear you admit it. Be willing to own up to your own faults and frailty.

When the fault is ours, we gain much respect and a quicker return to good favor when we respond immediately with regret for our part in the pain caused.

Just one more thing . . .

Ask yourself if there is someone you have injured
by your neglect or by self-absorbed thoughtlessness.
Determine to speak to that person or write a note
of apology this week.

_____

_____

_____

_____

_____

_____

_____

_____

_____

_____

_____

_____

Develop the ability to see life from the perspective of God's "big picture" and acknowledge that He is sovereign in all things.

Set your mind on the things above, not on the things that are on earth.   Colossians 3:2

By having a healthy, Christ-focused context for your life, you will be much better suited to handle disappointments, failures, and the various hard times that invariably come upon us all.

Rather than settling for a resigned, fatalistic view of life, you can know that your loving heavenly Father is in control. He is always at work in you to accomplish His greater purposes. Having this confidence in God brings encouragement, comfort, and keeps your heart and mind in balance when otherwise you would fall.

Just one more thing . . .

Consider one of your most recent disappointments. Instead of asking "Why me?", ask yourself "Why *not* me?" and see whether your perspective shifts. Write down any ideas you may have of what God's greater purposes might be for your life.

_____

_____

_____

_____

_____

_____

_____

_____

_____

_____

Avoid jumping to conclusions when you hear a "bad report" about someone. Choose instead to wait until you have checked out all the facts.

The first to plead his case seems just, until another comes and examines him.   Proverbs 18:17

All your life people will find ways to stir up trouble by telling you what someone said or what someone did. They will try to lead you to form an opinion that may not be supported by the facts. On other occasions, you will hear one side of a conversation, or one person's version of what was said or done, and be tempted to decide what to think about that person or situation. You will also be tempted to allow feelings to emerge that would be altered dramatically if you had the benefit of the entire conversation or if the whole situation was made known.

Gossip and rumors feed on half-truths, innuendos, and insinuation. Do not allow yourself to be manipulated by anything less than the truth, even when it is not immediately apparent what that truth might be. Frequently people tell you something bad about another person just to see if you know more than they do and if you can add to the poisonous pool they are filling.

Just one more thing . . .

When you sense that someone is telling you
something in an effort to draw forth some gossip
or rumor from you, do not be suckered into such a
ploy. Try to change the subject and get back to
a more positive topic if at all possible because
negativism only breeds more of the same.

_____

_____

_____

_____

_____

_____

_____

_____

_____

_____

Develop good habits in the areas of nourishment, rest, and exercise so that you will cultivate good physical health.

Or do you not know that your body is a temple of the Holy Spirit who is in you, whom you have from God, and that you are not your own? For you have been bought with a price: therefore glorify God in your body.
1 Corinthians 6:19–20

Discipline yourself for the purpose of godliness; for bodily discipline is only of little profit, but godliness is profitable for all things, since it holds promise for the present life and also for the life to come.
1 Timothy 4:7b–8

Decide now to cultivate good habits of physical health. Eating improperly (either too much, too little, or the wrong foods); sleeping unwisely (too much or too little); or exercising irregularly (too much or too little) will eventually weaken your physical health. As a result, your weakened physical condition can make you vulnerable spiritually as well. The discipline involved in making consistently good decisions about your physical health will also pay wonderful dividends when applied to your spiritual health.

Just one more thing...

Reflect on your personal habits this past week. Have you eaten properly, rested well, and exercised regularly? Determine what adjustments you need to make in your daily schedule. Then do it.

_____

_____

_____

_____

_____

_____

_____

_____

_____

_____

_____

_____

Never use the Scriptures to "bully" or manipulate others by trying to impress or intimidate them with your knowledge of the Bible.

And the Lord's bond-servant must not be quarrelsome, but be kind to all, able to teach, patient when wronged, with gentleness correcting those who are in opposition, if perhaps God may grant them repentance leading to the knowledge of the truth.   2 Timothy 2:24–25

The Bible is a sword, not a club, and its words pierce and cut with precision as the Holy Spirit takes the Word and applies it correctly. There is little eternal value in being right but for the wrong reasons. Be careful not to show off your knowledge to impress people with you instead of the Lord.

There is a danger in using the Word of God as a means to accomplish something or prove something when the desired result is to suit yourself. Instead, the Scriptures should be used to demonstrate concern for others and a desire for the glory of Christ.

Just one more thing . . .

Do you remember an incident when you attempted to impress others by your knowledge of the Bible? Ask God to forgive you and to help you treat others with gentleness and love instead.

Three down, one more to go!

Only one lap left with three successful laps behind you. By now, you know that you can do it! Once again, you do not want to miss the chance to congratulate each other by celebrating the completion of the third lap.

This time you might want to let your mom in on the celebration and take her along. She probably has all kinds of questions about what you two have been talking about. Perhaps you could share with her one of the best things you have learned so far or the idea that has hit home with you.

If for some reason mom is not able to go, maybe another dad and son you know would be encouraged to hear what you two have been doing. Ask them along to celebrate with you.

At any rate, this is a good time not only to enjoy your success thus far, but to share your experience with someone else.

Now, on to the last lap you go!

Never forget that God is more interested in how you make the journey rather than how quickly you arrive.

For this reason also, since the day we heard of it, we have not ceased to pray for you and to ask that you may be filled with the knowledge of His will in all spiritual wisdom and understanding, so that you may walk in a manner worthy of the Lord, to please Him in all respects, bearing fruit in every good work and increasing in the knowledge of God.
Colossians 1:9–10

As you pursue your goals and aspirations in life, remember that how you treat people along the way is more important than you may think. The presence or absence of a spirit of Christlikeness, the degree to which you become obsessed with reaching your temporal goal over your commitment to fulfill your eternal purpose of glorifying God—all of these measure the level of your spiritual maturity and your practical discernment about what really matters. People all around you will sell out to accomplish what they want. So love Christ more than anything else, and you will never sell out to anything or anyone but Him.

How you pursue your life goals matters more to the Lord than any earthly aspiration. Make your life's journey peacefully as you rest in the confidence that you are walking in step with the Spirit.

Just one more thing . . .

Look back over the past week or two. Are there
any incidents that reveal a tendency toward
headlong pursuit rather than mature discernment?

_____

_____

_____

_____

_____

_____

_____

_____

_____

_____

_____

_____

As a thermometer does not set the temperature but only reflects it, so the tongue does not determine our character but only reveals it.

Let no unwholesome word proceed from your mouth, but only such a word as is good for edification according to the need of the moment, that it may give grace to those who hear.   Ephesians 4:29

From the same mouth come both blessing and cursing. My brethren, these things ought not to be this way. Does a fountain send out from the same opening both fresh and bitter water?   James 3:10–11

If you find that you have trouble watching your language, the problem is probably not self-discipline but is more likely to be a problem with the character of your heart. The kind of attention you give to the development and nurture of your spiritual life will more than likely show up in the nature and content of your conversation.

Just one more thing . . .

If you keep having a problem with your words,
you probably need to pay more attention to what is
going on in your spiritual life. Keep track of what
you say this week and at the end of each day look
back to see if you used profane words, spoke
inappropriately to or about someone, or in other
ways allowed your lips to tear down instead of
build up the name of Christ.

_____

_____

_____

_____

_____

_____

_____

_____

Develop the habit of honoring and respecting women in general. Conduct yourself as a godly gentleman in their presence, valuing the unique differences God has chosen to establish between men and women.

You husbands likewise, live with your wives in an understanding way, as with a weaker vessel, since she is a woman; and grant her honor as a fellow heir of the grace of life, so that your prayers may not be hindered. 1 Peter 3:7

Rather than joking about or making fun of what you do not understand, learn to appreciate the valuable insights and complementary perspective women bring to any issue. Affirm the contributions they make and never act condescendingly toward them or generate an attitude that invites them to respond condescendingly toward you. Invite respect and honor by demonstrating both in the way you relate to women.

Just one more thing . . .

Think of a female teacher or a schoolmate you see
regularly throughout the week. What are some
ways you can show appropriate respect for her?

_____

_____

_____

_____

_____

_____

_____

_____

_____

_____

_____

W hen you talk to people, focus and look at *them,* not over or around them, as if you are looking for someone you consider to be more important.

For through the grace given to me I say to every man among you not to think more highly of himself than he ought to think; but to think so as to have sound judgment, as God has allotted to each a measure of faith ... Be devoted to one another in brotherly love; give preference to one another in honor. Romans 12:3,10

Have you ever been talking with someone when you noticed that they were neither listening to nor looking at you? Instead they kept looking over your shoulder in case they spotted someone else they would prefer to talk to rather than you. The message they were sending suggested that you were not important enough to receive their undivided attention. When Romans 12:10 says to "give preference to one another in honor," it literally means to outdo one another in showing honor.

Showing honor means not only listening attentively, but also finding other ways to communicate that this person is important to you. As a practical gesture, be sure to either shake this person's hand or in some other casual, but appropriate, manner, make contact with that person. Very few things will convey caring and warmth more than human touch. But be sensitive to the fact that it may make some people uncomfortable—honor this preference as well.

Just one more thing...

When you meet people this week, resolve to honor
them by making a connection with them in an
appropriate way, whether it is with a warm
handshake, a friendly smile, or by listening
attentively to them.

_____

_____

_____

_____

_____

_____

_____

_____

_____

_____

_____

Become an avid student of your moods and temperament so you can recognize negative trends and tendencies before they capture you in a trap of moody, self-absorbed behaviors and attitudes.

But now you also, put them all aside: anger, wrath, malice, slander, and abusive speech from your mouth. Do not lie to one another, since you laid aside the old self with its evil practices, and have put on the new self who is being renewed to a true knowledge according to the image of the One who created him. Colossians 3:8–10

Have this attitude in yourselves which was also in Christ Jesus.   Philippians 2:5

Once in a while everyone gets in a bad mood. The mark of growing maturity is to make sure that you do not give yourself permission to stay there. Often, nothing specific even prompts such moodiness. Don't allow yourself to descend too far into that dark hole—the deeper you go, the harder it is to crawl back out!

Just one more thing . . .

If you sense yourself beginning to develop a bad attitude this week, yield immediately to God's grace and mentally take a sharp turn in the opposite direction to get in step with the Lord and walk in the Spirit.

_____

_____

_____

_____

_____

_____

_____

_____

_____

_____

Don't allow yourself to be cynical. Instead learn to exercise discernment and good judgment before you decide *not* to trust someone.

Love does not delight in evil but rejoices with the truth. It always protects, always trusts, always hopes, always perseveres. 1 Corinthians 13:6–7 (NIV)

Someone once said that the moment we begin to be cynical is the moment we lose our youth. I would add that it is also the time we lose our ability to love unconditionally and freely in a Christlike manner, seeing people from His perspective. If you enter every relationship expecting to be disappointed in some way by the other person, you will nearly always be able to find something to prove that you are right.

How much better it is to meet others with a positive perspective and expect the best of them. If they sense that you trust them, they are much more likely to respond well and often will go to great lengths to live up to your confidence in them.

Just one more thing . . .

Think of a friendship in which you were disappointed.
Were your expectations of that friend reasonable?
How would you respond today if you had it to do
over again?

_____

_____

_____

_____

_____

_____

_____

_____

_____

_____

_____

_____

_____

_____

Maintain an attitude of sexual purity that governs the way you think and act when confronted with potentially compromising situations.

For this is the will of God, your sanctification; that is, that you abstain from sexual immorality; that each of you know how to possess his own vessel in sanctification and honor, not in lustful passion, like the Gentiles who do not know God.   1 Thessalonians 4:3–5

Establish unbreakable standards of behavior in your relationships with women that will protect you from falling into immorality and violating the sanctity of marriage. Set clearly defined limits beyond which you will *not* go and avoid situations that would encourage failure. Make it your commitment to choose to be only with women who share your commitment to godly purity in Jesus Christ, both as dating partners and ultimately marriage partners. Abstain from every kind of sexual immorality at all costs so that you may enter marriage as the man your Christlike bride desires and deserves.

Just one more thing . . .

Think of some situations that would make it
difficult for you to maintain your sexual purity.
How could you avoid them? Determine to do it.

_____

_____

_____

_____

_____

_____

_____

_____

_____

_____

_____

_____

_____

_____

A false witness, especially a lie or an attempt to deceive someone you love, pierces the soul like a knife and severs the delicate cords of trust upon which relationships depend.

Lying lips are an abomination to the LORD, but those who deal faithfully are His delight.   Proverbs 12:22

Therefore, laying aside falsehood, speak truth, each one of you, with his neighbor, for we are members of one another.   Ephesians 4:25

Relationships are built upon a foundation of trust. Whenever we undermine that foundation, the relationship always suffers.

A deceptive word or deed indicates that someone in the relationship does not know how the other person will respond to the truth. Eventually, discovery of the deception always comes, and the relationship is weakened.

Therefore, if you love someone, *never* deceive that person. It will only cause greater pain than the truth would have. The short-term relief that deception brings cannot compare with the long-term confidence that the truth will bring to your relationships.

Just one more thing . . .

Prayerfully determine before the Lord to always tell the truth—especially to those you love.

_____

_____

_____

_____

_____

_____

_____

_____

_____

_____

_____

_____

_____

Determine early in your life, before you are on your own financially, to adopt a lifestyle not controlled by materialism. Choose instead a lifestyle that is disciplined and restrained.

He who loves money will not be satisfied with money, nor he who loves abundance with its income. This too is vanity.   Ecclesiastes 5:10

Do not weary yourself to gain wealth, cease from your consideration of it. When you set your eyes on it, it is gone. For wealth certainly makes itself wings, like an eagle that flies toward the heavens.   Proverbs 23:4–5

Keep deception and lies far from me, give me neither poverty nor riches; feed me with the food that is my portion.   Proverbs 30:8

Since the overwhelming majority of people in our culture live well beyond their means, the temptation is to follow suit. Only a firm commitment (when you first begin supporting yourself) to live modestly and to avoid an excessive, lavish lifestyle will fight that temptation. Finding a wife who is committed to those same priorities is then a *must*, not just a pleasant option.

The most dangerous areas to get in financial trouble with include cars, your choice of housing, clothing, and entertainment/recreation preferences. There is such a wide range of available choices, and it is easy to bite off more than you can chew. Be wary of choosing a more opulent lifestyle to satisfy worldly drives for prestige, ease, recognition, acceptance, or other similar motivations.

Just one more thing . . .

Decide now to choose a simpler lifestyle even while you are still in school. Remember that prestige based on possessions is always shallow and short-lived.

_____

_____

_____

_____

_____

_____

_____

_____

_____

_____

M ake a "covenant with your eyes" and a commitment of your will to refrain from looking at or listening to things that defile and degrade your godly character.

I have made a covenant with my eyes; how then could I gaze at a virgin?   Job 31:1

I will set no worthless thing before my eyes; I hate the work of those who fall away; it shall not fasten its grip on me.   Psalm 101:3

All things are lawful, but not all things are profitable. All things are lawful, but not all things edify. 1 Corinthians 10:23

Opportunity has never been more abundant to introduce impure materials to your eyes and ears. Through motion pictures, video rentals, magazines, the Internet, cable television, and a host of other outlets, you have access to pornographic and morally repugnant resources unknown to previous generations. Private availability of such things has reduced the fear of exposure. As a result, much greater measures are needed to protect yourself against the intrusion of these threats to your purity.

Monitor the kinds of entertainment you tend to enjoy so that you do not gradually slip into unhealthy patterns of thought, which can sear your conscience. Reject things that growing, sensitive, and spiritually awakened Christians should find offensive. You do have freedom in Christ, but do not let that freedom turn into a license to ignore the propriety and purity that honor the Lord.

Just one more thing . . .

Are there some forms of entertainment in your life that might lead you into unhealthy thought patterns or dull your sensitivity to the Holy Spirit?

_____

_____

_____

_____

_____

_____

_____

_____

_____

_____

_____

When your anger is aroused, treat it with great caution so that it does not control you and find unacceptable expression.

Be angry, and yet do not sin; do not let the sun go down on your anger, and do not give the devil an opportunity. Ephesians 4:26–27

An angry man stirs up strife, and a hot-tempered man abounds in transgression.   Proverbs 29:22

It's easy to get angry for lots of reasons—sports, relationships, you name it. We need to develop ways to identify our anger and then examine and analyze its character to see if it is righteous and just or not. If it is righteous, then we should redirect the anger in a manner consistent with our new life in Christ.

Be especially careful in what you say or do when you realize that your anger has gotten the best of you. No profane words, violent actions, or hasty reactions will provide the kind of outlet for satisfactory relief that taking it to Christ will. As difficult as it is, Jesus wants us to understand that we do not have to follow our anger with sin if we will take it to Him first.

Just one more thing . . .

Do you remember the last time you became really angry? Was your anger justified or not?
How could you have been "angry without sin"?

_____

_____

_____

_____

_____

_____

_____

_____

_____

_____

_____

_____

_____

Give thanks by expressing it, both to the Lord and to others, on a regular basis.

The lines have fallen to me in pleasant places; indeed, my heritage is beautiful to me.   Psalm 16:6

Enter His gates with thanksgiving, and His courts with praise. Give thanks to Him; bless His name. Psalm 100:4

I thank my God in all my remembrance of you. Philippians 1:3

Once in a while, take time to remember those individuals who have made a difference in your life and find a way to communicate your gratitude to them. Take care not to take for granted the blessings you enjoy.

Ask the Lord to show you something new every day for which you can thank Him. You will then grow in your awareness of the faithfulness of your heavenly Father. An old hymn advises us to "count your many blessings, name them one by one, and it will surprise you what the Lord has done." Giving thanks on a consistent basis will help you to become a genuinely grateful person.

Just one more thing . . .

Identify someone who made the extra effort to do
something kind for you recently. What can you
do to express your gratitude to that person?

_____

_____

_____

_____

_____

_____

_____

_____

_____

_____

_____

_____

Surround yourself with people who are more loyal to Christ and His Word than to you.

Faithful are the wounds of a friend, but deceitful are the kisses of an enemy.   Proverbs 27:6

People tend to surround themselves with "yes-men," rather than with people who will challenge, confront, and hold them accountable to their commitments. As believers, we need friends who will help us to walk with Christ with integrity. Therefore, cultivate friendships and relationships with people who are more committed to Christ than they are to making you feel good or trying to say and do what you want.

If the companions you seek in life love you faithfully, in a Christlike manner, their first loyalty will be to Him and to seeing His life demonstrated through you. They will not be afraid to say what needs to be said in order to encourage you to walk in a manner worthy of the Lord.

Rather than have well-intentioned but ungodly acquaintances who care more what *you* think than what *Christ* thinks, it is far better to have friends who will challenge you when you make wrong choices, confront you when you sin, and counsel you to make the right decisions.

Just one more thing . . .

Reflect on your friendships and name one or two people who love Christ and love you enough to tell you the truth about yourself. Is there someone you have turned away from because he spoke the truth and you did not like it? What can you do to restore or cultivate friendships like these this week?

_____

_____

_____

_____

_____

_____

_____

_____

_____

_____

_____

You Did It!

I pray that these 52 weeks have drawn you together as two seeking the Father's best in your lives. As you look back over the year's successes and failures, you have grown as you went through them together. Many of your experiences had nothing to do with the content of this book but grew out of the character of your relationship.

What can you do next? How will you sustain some of the momentum you have gained? What will you do to see that others benefit from what you have shared as a father and son?

Do not pass up this last opportunity to mark this milestone by celebrating with great joy what God has taught you both. Be creative in coming up with something good to recognize and value what the Lord has allowed you to share.

In closing, I leave you with these words from Solomon to his son in Proverbs:

> *My son, if you will receive my words and treasure my commandments within you, make your ear attentive to wisdom, incline your heart to understanding; for if you cry for discernment, lift your voice for understanding; if you seek her as silver and search for her as for hidden treasures; then you will discern the fear of the Lord and discover the knowledge of God. For the Lord gives wisdom; from His mouth come knowledge and understanding. He stores up sound wisdom for the upright; He is a shield to those who walk in integrity, guarding the paths of justice, and He preserves the way of His godly ones. Then you will discern righteousness and justice and equity and every good*

course. For wisdom will enter your heart and knowledge will be pleasant to your soul; discretion will guard you, understanding will watch over you.

Trust in the Lord with all your heart and do not lean on your own understanding. In all your ways acknowledge Him, and He will make your paths straight.

Proverbs 2:1–11; 3:5–6

As you close this last session in prayer, give thanks to the Lord for His wisdom in showing you His ways.

—————•◊◊•—————

Just one more thing . . .

"Trust in the Lord and do good; dwell in the land and enjoy safe pasture. Delight yourself in the Lord and He will give you the desires of your heart."

Psalm 37:3–4, NIV